PAINTING FROM THE
PALETTE OF LOVE

PAINTING from the PALETTE of LOVE

The Mystical Poetry of
KABIR

THOMAS RAIN CROWE

SHAMBHALA

Shambhala Publications, Inc.
2129 13th Street
Boulder, Colorado 80302
www.shambhala.com

Cover art: Anna Pogulyaeva/Shutterstock.com
Cover & interior design: Kate E. White

9 8 7 6 5 4 3 2 1

First Edition
Printed in the United States of America

Shambhala Publications makes every
effort to print on acid-free, recycled paper.
Shambhala Publications is distributed worldwide by
Penguin Random House, Inc., and its subsidiaries.

LIBRARY OF CONGRESS CATALOGING-IN-PUBLICATION DATA
Names: Crowe, Thomas Rain, author. | Kabir, active 15th century.
Title: Painting from the palette of love: the mystical poetry of Kabir /
versions by Thomas Rain Crowe.
Description: Boulder: Shambhala, 2023.
Identifiers: LCCN 2022041896 | ISBN 9781645471868 (trade paperback)
Subjects: LCSH: Kabir, active 15th century—Sources. |
Hinduism—Poetry. | Religious poetry, Hindi.
Classification: LCC PS3553.R5924 P35 2023 | DDC 811/.54—dc23/eng/20230217
LC record available at https://lccn.loc.gov/2022041896

For Qahira and for Robert Bly,
who took me there.

Contents

Introduction

1

PART ONE: He

11   Where My Beloved Lives
12   The Breath of Wind inside the Wind
13   Between the Known and the Unknown
14   Castles Made of Sand
15   No Tour Guide
16   Wake Up!
17   The Stigma of Death
18   The Ocean of Life

19 This Small Clay Bowl

20 The Secret Word

21 Dancing in the Light of Love

22 The Bird of Paradise

23 The Light of Love

24 That Foreign Shore

25 Illusion

26 The True Path

27 The Land of No Sorrow

28 The Face of Fulfilled Desire

29 In My Body

30 Faith

31 The Garden of Flowers

32 All the Same

33 Knowing the Unknown

34 Suffering

35 Grieving

36 The Beloved's Song

37 Lost Love

38 What Is Real

39 Painting with the Palette of Love

40 The Message

41 The Wine of the Beloved

PART TWO: She

45   If You Don't Even Know Your Own God

46   Patience

47   Fear

48   The Land of Death

49   The Sound of Her Flute

50   The Jewel

51   Light

52   A Million Suns

53   Neither/Nor

54   The Nothing and the Everything

55   The Beloved Is One

56   The Beloved Beggar

57   Good Luck

58   Clouds in the Sky

59   What a Wonderful Day

60   Imagined Joy

61   Pride and Vanity

62   The Spinning Wheel

63   Crying without Tears

64   Why Are You Asleep

65   Spring

66   The Swing of Love

67   Dancing in Ecstasy

68   What Is the Need of Words?

69   Like the River Flows to the Ocean

70   The Battlefield of the Body

71   At Home

72   The Best Kind of Love

73   There Is Nothing but Water in the Pool

74   A Tree with No Name

75   The Word

76   The Ocean of Happiness

77   Free of Pride and Conceit

78   Old Habits

Acknowledgments

79

About the Author

81

PAINTING FROM THE
PALETTE OF LOVE

Introduction

My introduction to Sufi poetry was through Robert Bly. I heard him read his versions of Kabir in San Francisco when I was living there in the 1970s. Soon after that I bought his *Kabir Book: Forty-Four of the Ecstatic Poems of Kabir* at the neighborhood used bookstore in North Beach. Some years later I married a woman from North Carolina who was an ordained Sufi *mureed* (disciple) and I was thrown into the world of American Sufism in a major way—which included becoming familiar with Sufi practices as well as Sufi masters and poets from the present and the past. Since those years, I have been an avid student of the Sufi, Stoic, and Buddhist traditions, following more intensely the poetry coming from these spiritual contexts, including the works of Marcus Aurelius, Rumi, Hafiz, and Kabir. And it is to Kabir that I have given my full attention most recently.

Kabir was originally known as Kabir Das (1398–1455). From all we know, Kabir was a simple man and not actually a practicing ascetic, as such, but a regular family man and part of a community where he was a weaver by vocation. When he died, both Hindus and Muslims claimed him as their own. Kabir believed that spiritual wisdom—or "Truth," as he called it—was only available to the person who is on the path to the Divine and not confined to the material or mental aspects of the world. To know the Truth, Kabir said, one must drop the ego. Kabir's legacy continues to be kept alive by those in the religious community based on his teachings known as the Kabir Panth, or "Path of Kabir," of which adherents are known as Kabir panthis.

Kabir is widely believed to have become one of the many disciples of the bhakti poet-saint Swami Ramananda, known for the devotional teaching that God is inside every person and every thing. Early texts about Kabir's life place him within the Vaishnava tradition of Hinduism as well as the Sufi tradition of Islam. Kabir composed his verses using simple Hindi words. Most of his work concerns devotion, mysticism, and discipline. Kabir and his followers named his poems of wisdom, which include songs and couplets, *banis*. The term *bani* means "utterance" but also "witness," implying that the poems testify to the Truth.

Kabir's poems were verbally composed in the fifteenth century and transmitted orally, written down for the first time in the seventeenth century. Scholars say that this form of transmission, across geography and generations, led to interpolation and corruption of the original poems. Whole songs were fabricated and new couplets inserted by unknown authors and attributed to Kabir—not because of dishonesty but out of respect for him and to participate in the creative project of Indian oral literature. Thus, it is difficult to ascertain which lines of verse truly come from Kabir.

Kabir's poetry almost ridicules man's need for religion, citing many of the religions of his day. Rather than rituals and strict doctrines, Kabir encouraged his followers to "go within" and to consider oneself as being part and parcel of God.

In the first quarter of the twentieth century, the Indian scholar Kshitimohan Sen compiled many dozens of poems to which Kabir's name is attached from mendicants and manuscripts across India, sifting out the spurious ones and publishing those he deemed authentic in Hindi and Bengali. Rabindranath Tagore (1861–1941)—Indian poet, philosopher, and artist—used Sen's publication as the basis of his *Songs of Kabir* (1915), selecting one hundred of the poems and translating them into English for the first time.

Of these, I have chosen sixty-five, interpreting and rendering them into a contemporary framework and language, making them accessible to a modern-day readership looking to non-Western spiritualities for inspiration. And at this time in which traditional gender roles are being examined ever more critically, I took particular care to make the poems accessible to women, in part by using feminine pronouns for God in the entire second half of the book.

The poems I have chosen for this book are the more mystical, and one might also say the more self-help-oriented, poems. As I've said, my versions are infused with modern references and in a modern vernacular. My approach in this regard is much the same as that of the Indian poet Arvind Krishna Mehrotra in his *Songs of Kabir* translations (2011), as he uses contemporary equivalents of Kabir's phrases to appeal to a modern audience (using the name of an actual modern-day American prison, for instance, instead of referring simply to "criminals"). I have done similar things with my renditions, which bring to bear language that both transcends and includes the traditional gender binary—allowing the mystical implications of Kabir's theology to shine through. God, the Beloved, is thus depicted as Him, Her, and ultimately beyond such conventional language. Among my influences are the style of Robert Bly and the translations of Tagore along with Bly's methods of modernization with regard to voice and language. In this sense this collection is a confluence of Tagore, Bly, and Thomas Rain Crowe.

In rendering Kabir's poems into a modern vernacular, I am also trying to preserve their mystical qualities and teachings. Although not identified as such, there is much of the Stoic philosophy in his work, which first arose in the early third century BCE. Stoicism is a philosophy of personal virtue ethics—highlighting the virtues of courage, temperance, justice, and wisdom—informed by a logic-based system of living in accordance with the natural world that is designed to make us more resilient, happier, and wiser. Over time, many of the world's great leaders, spiritual masters, and artists were influenced by Stoic philosophy, as exemplified by such famous adages as "Don't explain your philosophy; embody it" (Epictetus) and "If it is not right, do not do it; if it is not true, do not say it" (Marcus Aurelius). In making my selections for this volume, I have chosen poems that I think are not only "mystical" but that are also in line with the enlightened thinking of Kabir's time and embraced by the Sufi spiritual movement as well as by the older Stoic line of thinking and acting. In the past I have done something very similar with the poems of Hafiz, based on the work of nineteenth-century British translator Henry Wilberforce Clarke, in *Drunk on the Wine of the Beloved: 100 Poems of Hafiz* (2001) and *In Wineseller's Street* (1998), focusing on his ecstatic "wine" poems. Here I have likewise tried to emphasize an ecstatic mystical message that has meaning and practical applications for all people. When Kabir writes,

> You won't find me in shrines or in stupas;
> Not in masses, nor with legs curled around my neck,
> Nor in some fancy restaurant.
> If you are really looking for me, I am not hard to find—
> You will find me in some tiny house of Time.
> Kabir says: O student, tell me, what is God?
> He is the breath of wind inside the wind.

he is telling you exactly what he thinks, what he thinks you should be thinking, and where you should be looking to find yourself on the higher road to self and spiritual awareness and consciousness.

While I am not the only person doing modern English versions of Kabir's poetry, I am doing them in a particular way that is as true as possible both to Tagore's literal translations and to my own personal knowledge and experience of Sufi traditions, Eastern and Western. Kabir's poems and his message are so essential right now—in terms of not only our mental and physical health but our very survival. As the cultural historian and "geologian" Thomas Berry says, "It will take a conversion experience deep in the psychic structure of the human to get things back on track and moving toward finding ourselves in a state of balance with the natural world and the universe." In other words, there is still hope if we will take the time to focus and learn from the real teachers. I think there is always room for new translations of a great poet.

PART ONE

He

WHERE MY BELOVED LIVES

There is no happiness or unhappiness.
There is no truth and no lies.
There is no sin and no virtue.
There is no day or night, no sun or moon.
There is only radiance and the absence of light.
There is no meditation or knowledge.
There are no mantras or innocuous prayers.
There is no speech coming from the Vedas or foreign books.
All this is lost in this place.
No inside, no outside, no home or homeless.
The very small and the very large do not exist.
Neither the elements of the periodic table
Nor the holy trinity are there.
Even Silence is not there.
No roots, no flowers, no branches, no seeds.
But even without a tree the fruits abound;
There is only the breath of wind that sounds like "Om."
Here, the lists of life are nowhere to be found.
There is absolutely nothing where the Beloved exists.
Kabir says: I know what I know,
And whoever reads my poems will become free.

THE BREATH OF WIND INSIDE THE WIND

I've got your back.
You won't find me in shrines or in stupas;
Not in masses, nor with legs curled around my neck,
Nor in some fancy restaurant.
If you are really looking for me, I am not hard to find—
You will find me in some tiny house of Time.
Kabir says: O student, tell me, what is God?
He is the breath of wind inside the wind.

BETWEEN THE KNOWN AND THE UNKNOWN

Between the known and the unknown
The mind has put up a swing:
A playground for all beings and all worlds,
All swinging.
Everyone is swinging, even the sun and moon.
Millennia pass by, and this goes on . . .
Everyone is swinging! The earth, the air, the water,
And the Beloved Himself.
Kabir saw this and it made him a servant for life!

CASTLES MADE OF SAND

I have been studying the difference
Between the water and the waves.
When the water rises, it is still water.
When the water crashes, it is still water.
Please, give me a hint.
How does one tell them apart?
Because there is the word "water,"
What makes it different from a wave?
Inside us, a Secret One resides.
The planets in all the galaxies
Pass through His hands like sand.
Kabir says: What kind of sandcastle
Will you build with your hands?

NO TOUR GUIDE

I said to the greedy person inside me:
What is this river you want to cross?
There are no nomads or migrants on the road and no road.
Do you see anyone resting over there on that bank?
There is no river at all, no boat and no boatman.
There is no towrope or no tour guide.
There is no ground, no sky, no time, no bank, and no bridge.
And there is not even a body or a mind!
Knowing this, do you still believe
That there is a place that will satisfy your desires?
If so, you will never find it.
So be strong and stay inside your own body;
Your hands and feet have a welcome mat there.
Think about this.
Don't go off looking for somewhere else.
Kabir says: Do away with all unnecessary thoughts
And stand strong in who you are.

WAKE UP!

O mourning heart,
Wake up! The Master is very near.
So run to the feet of the Beloved.
You have been asleep for a million lifetimes
And it is time, now, for you to wake.

THE STIGMA OF DEATH

The lights are on in every house.
O blind one, you cannot see them.
But maybe one day your eyes will open
And the stigma of death will fall away
And you will be able to see.
There is nothing for you to say, hear, or do.
He who is both living and dead will never die again.

THE OCEAN OF LIFE

Living alone in a cave, the yogi
Tells his students that his home is far away.
Why do you climb tall trees in order to see the Beloved?
He is standing right behind your back.
The Brahman priest goes from house to house
Converting people to his faith:
So why have you set up an altar where you can pray?
The true ocean of life is right there under your feet.
Kabir says: I can't put into words how special the Beloved is.
All the prayer beads and all the yoga in the world
Mean nothing to Him.

THIS SMALL CLAY BOWL

In this small clay bowl are fields and forests.
It is there that the Creator resides.
Within this bowl are the seven oceans
And all the stars in the sky.
The sacred earth and the environmentalist live there too.
In this bowl the sound of Eternity sings,
As does the sacred spring.
Kabir says: Listen to me, my friend:
The Beloved lives inside of you!

THE SECRET WORD

How can I even utter the Secret Word?
How can I say that He is like this or He is like that?
If I say that He is within me, the universe will be offended.
If I say that He is outside me, I know this will be a lie.
The Beloved has created the inside and outside worlds as One.
He has two stools on which to rest
His conscious and unconscious minds.
He is neither visible nor invisible,
He is neither here nor there.
Kabir says: There are not enough words to describe
Who He really is.

DANCING IN THE LIGHT OF LOVE

I have been playing day and night with my friends.
So much play, and now I am lost.
The Beloved's palace is so high in the sky
That I am afraid to even climb the stairs.
But if I stay here on this ground, I will never know His love.
So I must take off my veil of fear and give Him a hug.
And I must dance in the higher heavens in the light of Love.
Kabir says: Listen to me, my friend.
If you don't feel any longing for the Beloved,
It is a waste of time to go out and buy new clothes,
Put on perfume, or paint mascara on your eyes.

THE BIRD OF PARADISE

O Bird of Paradise, tell me about your life.
Where do you come from? Where are you going?
And where would you go to die?
Tell me, what is it you are looking for?
This morning I awoke and thought:
"O Bird of Paradise, take flight and follow me."
I know a land where there is no doubt or sorrow,
And where death does not reside.
There it is springtime and flowers are in full bloom.
And the scent of the Beloved is blowing in the wind.
Kabir says: The bee of my heart lives in His flower
And knows only of His joy.

THE LIGHT OF LOVE

O Beloved, who will serve You?
With everyone paying homage to gods
They have created for themselves,
No one is seeking You.
They may believe in ten avatars,
But no avatar can hold a candle to You.
Those who worship false idols will only suffer
The results of their own confusion.
You are better than this.
Meanwhile, the yogis, the saints, and every priest
Argue over whose god is real.
Kabir says: Only he who has seen
The light of Love can be saved.

THAT FOREIGN SHORE

It is springtime and the Garden Goddess
Is singing her favorite song.
Here, light shines in all directions,
And there are few who can afford to pay the boatman
To get them to that foreign shore.
There, there are millions of Krishnas,
And millions of Vishnus who bow their heads.
Millions of Brahmans are reading the Vedas,
Millions of Shivas are lost in prayer,
Millions of angels live in the sky,
Stone statues and false idols are countless,
And millions of Saraswatis play beautiful tunes on their harps.
Kabir says: It is here that you can find the Beloved.
You can smell His fragrance in the woods.

ILLUSION

Tell me, my friend, how can I get rid of all this illusion?
When I gave up tying pretty bows around packages,
I still tied my pants up with a string.
And when I gave up tying up my pants,
I still wore shirts that didn't fit.
When I gave up my sexual longings,
I found that I was angry all day.
And when I gave up my anger,
I became even more greedy than before.
Even when I was able to get rid of my greed,
Pride and vanity took its place.
When the mind is empty
And illusion is thrown away,
It still hangs on to one thing.
Kabir says: Listen to what I have to say:
There are very few who find their way.

THE TRUE PATH

The True Path is like a labyrinth.
On this path there are no questions and no answers.
The ego simply has to disappear.
The joy of looking for the Beloved
Is like the ocean, and you just have to dive in
And swim around like a fish in water.
Kabir says: If anyone should need anything,
The Lover leaps up from the water
And gives them what they need.

THE LAND OF NO SORROW

Traveling by no road, I have come to the Land of No Sorrow.
How easily the spirit of the Beloved has come to me.
People talk of Him as being infinite and unattainable,
But in my meditations, I have seen Him with closed eyes.
This is indeed the Land of No Sorrow,
And no one knows which road to take to get there.
Only he who is on this path has truly transcended all pain.
How wonderful is that land of rest that is not for sale.
It is only the wise ones who have been there
And only the wise ones who have sung its songs.
No words can come close to describing this kind of calm.
Only those who have experienced this calm
Can know it and know its joy.
Kabir says: Knowing this, an ignorant man becomes wise
And a wise man becomes deaf and mute.

THE FACE OF FULFILLED DESIRE

O friends, search for the Beloved while you are still alive.
Jump into this experience!
And be mindful—while you are still alive!
What people sometimes refer to as "salvation"
All happens before you die.
If you don't break these worldly ties while you're alive,
Who do you think is going to help you when you're dead?
The idea that the soul will unite with God
Just because the body has decayed is all fantasy.
What you know now is what you'll know then.
If you know nothing now,
You will simply end up with an empty apartment
In the City of Death.
But if you make love to the Beloved now,
In your next life you will have the smile of fulfilled desire.
So dive into that stream of wisdom
And find who the true Teacher is,
And believe in the song of Truth.
Kabir says: O student, when searching for the Beloved,
It is the intensity of your longing that is doing all the work.
Just look at me and you will see a slave of that intensity.

IN MY BODY

The moon shines in my body,
But I can't see it if I am blind.
The moon is in my body, but so is the sun.
My heartbeat is a drum,
But I cannot hear it with deaf ears.
When your love for what is "me" and "mine" is dead,
That is when the Beloved's work is done.
For knowledge is the wise man's work.
And when that comes, all other work is put up on the shelf.
Kabir says: The flower blooms for the fruit;
When the fruit is ripe, the flower dies.

FAITH

Where are you looking for Me?
I am with you, my friend.
Not in prayers or meditations.
Not in fasting.
Not in yogic postures.
Not in renunciation.
Not in New Age books or even in the body.
And not even in infinite space.
Not in the womb of nature.
Not in the breath inside the breath.
So seek and search sincerely.
It will only take you a second.
Kabir says: Listen to what I say:
Where your trust resides, it is there that you will find your God.

THE GARDEN OF FLOWERS

Do not go into the garden of flowers!
No, do not go there.
The garden of flowers is in your body.
Sit down on nature's mirror,
And look there upon the infinite beauty that is you!

ALL THE SAME

You don't need to ask a saint which caste he belongs to.
For the priest, the general, the carpenter, and all thirty-six
Castes are all looking for God.
The hairdresser and the maid are looking too.
Everyone, from all castes, is making this pilgrimage.
Hindus, Muslims, Buddhists, and Christians
Have all made this journey and they are all the same.

KNOWING THE UNKNOWN

It is because my true Guru is merciful
That I have come to know the unknown.
I have learned from Him how to walk without feet,
To see without eyes, to hear without ears,
To drink without lips, and to fly without wings.
I have brought my love into a land where
There is no sun or moon, no day or night.
Without eating anything, I have tasted the sweetness of honey;
And without water, I have quenched my thirst.
Where there is joy, there is the fullness of delight.
To whom should I address that joy?
Kabir says: The Guru is great beyond words;
How lucky can His disciple be!

SUFFERING

I want to see my Beloved!
I've suffered from pain both day and night and I cannot sleep.
It's time for me to move out of my parent's house.
The door of the sky has opened to me
And it is my Beloved's house that now I see.
There I will find my soulmate, and at His feet
I will leave the offering of my body and my mind.

GRIEVING

My body and my mind are grieving and are missing You.
O Beloved, come over to my house.
When my friends tell me that I am Your bride,
I feel ashamed; for I cannot feel You with my hands.
So, what is this love of mine? I can't eat, I can't sleep,
And my heart is restless when I'm inside
And when I'm out-of-doors.
Like water is to someone with great thirst,
So the lover is to the bride.
So, who is going to take this news to my Beloved?
Kabir says: Right now, I just want to see His face.

THE BELOVED'S SONG

My body is His harp.
He tightens the strings and from these strings
Comes the melody of God.
If the strings should break and the keys go flat,
Then back to dust will this instrument of dust return.
Kabir says: Only the Beloved can play this song.

LOST LOVE

Lost love shuts the metal gate.
The key of Love opens it again.
From the sound of the gate opening, the Beloved will awake.
Kabir says: Do not let a chance like this go by!

WHAT IS REAL

I am laughing at the story of the thirsty fish in the water.
Can't you see that what is real is right there in your home?
Why do you wander aimlessly from place to place?
Kabir will tell you the truth: Go anywhere, to India or to Nepal;
If you do not find your soul, the world will always seem unreal.

PAINTING WITH THE PALETTE OF LOVE

I have calmed my restless mind, and my heart is beating again:
For in this Otherness I have seen beyond Otherness,
And in good company I have seen Him there.
I was living in my own prison, but have set myself free
And have escaped from the laws of ignorance.
Kabir says: I have attained the impossible,
And my heart is now painted from the palette of Love.

THE MESSAGE

O, I am so desperate to meet the Beloved!
I am no longer young, and the pain of separation from Him
Troubles my sleep.
Still lost on the back roads of knowledge,
In my dreams I have received His news.
I have gotten a message from Him.
In this message is the key to life,
And so now my fear of death has gone away.
Kabir says: How lucky I am! I have received this gift
From the One Who Does Not Die.

THE WINE OF THE BELOVED

O drunken friend, empty your cup!
Drink, instead, the wine of the Beloved!
Kabir says: Listen to me, I will tell you the truth.
You are poisoning your mind with all that cheap beer—
From the soles of your feet to the top of your head.
Drink the wine in the Beloved's cup.
His vintage wine will free your mind
And fill your heart with grace.

PART TWO

She

IF YOU DON'T EVEN KNOW YOUR OWN GOD

If you don't even know your own god,
How can you have such a huge ego?
Put your selfishness away.
Your words are not suited for a saint.
And don't be deceived by reading the scriptures:
Love is something more important than this.
Kabir says: He who seeks Her love will find himself.

PATIENCE

O humans, why are you so impatient?
She who watches over birds, beasts, and insects,
She who cared for you
When you were still in your mother's womb,
Would She not care for you now?
O humans,
How could you turn away from the smile of the Beloved
And wander so far away from Her?
You have left your Beloved and are thinking only of yourself,
And this is why all your work seems so fruitless and in vain.

FEAR

How hard it is to meet the Beloved!
The rain-crow cries in thirst for the rain.
She almost dies of her own desire,
Yet she will drink nothing but the rain.
Drawn by the love of music, the minstrel walks in the woods.
He will die listening to this music, but he will not die in fear.
The widow sits by the body of her dead husband,
But she is not afraid of the funeral pyre.
Kabir says: Put away all fear for your body
And play new songs on the Beloved's harp.

THE LAND OF DEATH

The yogi dyes his garments
Instead of dyeing his mind with the colors of love.
He sits in the temple worshipping a stone.
He pierces holes in his ears and has a long beard,
Matted hair, and looks like a goat.
He even goes out into the wilderness to get rid of his desires
And becomes celibate.
He shaves his head and dyes his garments again.
He reads the Bhagavad Gita and talks to great crowds.
Kabir says: O yogi, you are headed to the land of death,
Bound hand and foot!

THE SOUND OF HER FLUTE

I can hear the sound of Her flute!
I can't control myself!
It is not spring yet, but the flowers are blooming;
And already the bees are here.
The sky is howling and the thunder is booming,
And ocean waves rise up in my heart.
The rain finally comes and I long for my Beloved.
The rhythms of the world rise and fall like the beat of my heart,
Where the flags of nations are fluttering in the air.
Kabir says: My heart is dying, but it lives!

THE JEWEL

The Jewel is lost in the mud,
And everyone is searching for it.
Some look for it in the east, and some in the west;
Some in the water, and some amongst the stones.
Kabir, the servant, has appraised the Jewel
At its true value, and has wrapped it with care
And placed it on the mantle of his heart.

LIGHT

The Vedas say that the Unconditioned
Lies beyond the world of Conditions.
O, why do you want to argue
Whether She is beyond all or in all?
Instead, see everything as the place where you reside—
A place where there is no pleasure and no pain.
There, Brahma is revealed both night and day.
There, light is Her garment. And light is Her chair.
Kabir says: She is the true Master and is nothing but light.

A MILLION SUNS

Let's go to that country where the Beloved lives,
She who has stolen my heart!
There, Love is filling Her bucket from the well,
Yet She has no rope to pull the bucket out.
In that country, there are no clouds in the sky,
Yet we still get gentle rain.
O friend, don't just sit there on your couch;
Go out and take a bath in that rain!
In that country there is always moonlight and it is never dark.
And who is spreading the fake news that there is only one sun?
The Land of the Beloved is brightened
With the rays of a million suns!

NEITHER/NOR

I am neither God-fearing nor ungodly.
I live neither by law nor by common sense alone.
I am neither a talker nor a listener.
I am neither a master nor a slave.
I am neither imprisoned nor free.
I am neither detached nor attached.
I am neither married nor single.
I am not going to heaven or to hell.
I can create great works, yet I can create much kitsch.
Very few understand me, and he who can doesn't care.
Kabir seeks neither to create nor to destroy.

THE NOTHING AND THE EVERYTHING

The Beloved doesn't eat and doesn't drink,
And neither lives nor dies:
She has neither color, line, form, nor fame.
For someone like Her who has no caste or clan,
How can I even begin to describe Her light?
She even has no name!
She has neither color nor colorlessness,
And is homeless—has no place to live.
Kabir says: She who has neither caste nor country,
Who is formless and defies description, fills all space.

THE BELOVED IS ONE

The Beloved is One. She is life and death,
Union and separation. All these are Her actions and Her joy.
She plays on the land and in the water, and the whole universe!
She plays on the earth and in the sky!
When She plays, Creation grows.
Kabir says: The whole world is Her playground,
Yet still we don't even know Her name.

THE BELOVED BEGGAR

The Beloved Beggar is out and begging,
But I couldn't even catch sight of Her:
And what can I beg of the Beggar if I did?
She gives me what I want before I even ask.
Kabir says: She owns me.
And I have given myself away.

GOOD LUCK

Obey your Beloved, who has come into this church of life!
Don't be an idiot, for night is coming and it's almost dark.
She has waited for me now all these years,
Yet I did not know She was waiting or of Her grace,
For my love was still asleep.
But now She has shown me the meaning
Of the secret note that found my ear:
And from this perfect pitch my good fortune has come!
Kabir says: I am awake and am grateful for my good luck.
I have received endless kisses from my Beloved!

CLOUDS IN THE SKY

Today there are clouds in the sky!
Listen to their howling and their deep voice.
The rain comes today from the east in a cloudy mist.
Take care of the fences and the boundaries of your fields,
Prepare the soil of awakening, and let the insects of love
And denial be soaked in this shower.
It is the wise farmer who will be able to bring his harvest home.
He will fill his bowls,
And then feed both the wise men and the saints.

WHAT A WONDERFUL DAY

Today is a day of celebration,
For today the Beloved One is a guest in my house
And my home is beautiful with Her presence.
My desires call Her name, and they are lost in Her love:
So I wash Her feet and I look up at Her face;
And I lay before Her in the grass, and as an offering
I give up my body, my mind, and all that I possess.
What a wonderful day this is!
My Beloved has come to my house!
Everything fearful and negative leaves my heart when I see Her.
Kabir says: My heart longs for the Name that is Truth,
And I can be a servant to all slaves.

IMAGINED JOY

Where can I go to learn about the Beloved?
Kabir says: Just like you won't find the forest
If you ignore the trees, so you won't find Her
In abstract art or imagined joy.

PRIDE AND VANITY

I have learned Sanskrit and now all men think I'm wise;
But how can I use this when I am floating adrift,
Parched with thirst, and burning with the heat of desire?
It is a total waste of time to take on a life of pride and vanity.
Kabir says: Lay all this down in the dust,
And then go to meet the Beloved,
And address Her as your Master and your Love.

THE SPINNING WHEEL

The woman who is parted from her lover
Spins at the spinning wheel.
The wheel of Love turns in the sky,
And the seat is made of diamonds and of knowledge.
Such subtle yarns the woman spins,
That will become clothes and rugs with love and reverence!
Kabir says: I am weaving the warp and weft of day and night.
When my Lover comes and touches my feet,
I will repay Her with my tears.

CRYING WITHOUT TEARS

O Beloved, my country is without sorrow.
I cry without tears—to the king and the beggar,
The president and the poet,
And anyone who needs shelter in Her love.
They are all welcome in my land!
Let the homeless and the heathens come here
And lay their burdens down!
You can live here too, my sister,
So that you may cross easily to that other shore.
It is a land without earth or sky, without moon or stars.
Only the radiance of Truth shines on my Beloved's beach.
Kabir says:
O friends, everything is worthless till you know the Truth.

WHY ARE YOU ASLEEP

O friend, listen to what I have to say.
If you are the lover you say you are,
Then why are you asleep?
If you have found the Beloved,
Then give yourself up completely
And take Her to your heart while you are still awake.
Why do you keep losing Her again and again?
If all you want to do is sleep,
Then why do you waste your time
Making the bed and arranging the pillows?
Kabir says: I'm going to tell you about Love.
Even though you think you've been given the shaft,
Don't sit around all day and cry.

SPRING

The month of March is here,
And who will take me to my Lover?
I can't even find words to describe the beauty of my Beloved,
For She is part of all that is beautiful.
She is the pigment in every painting in the world,
And this boggles the mind.
The few that know this understand the magic of Spring.
Kabir says: Listen to me, my friend, and don't be sad.
There are very few who understand.

THE SWING OF LOVE

Hang up the swing of Love today!
Hang your body and your mind
Between the arms of the Beloved,
And swing in the ecstasy of Love's joy.
Bring that tear-filled rain from the clouds
To your eyes, and cover your heart with the shadow of night.
Go, now, and whisper in Her ear,
And tell Her of the desperate longing of your heart.
Kabir says: Listen to me!
Show me how you and the Beloved are forever wed.

DANCING IN ECSTASY

Dance, O my heart! Dance today with joy!
The sound of love is filling my days and nights with music,
And the whole world is listening to its melodies:
Both life and death are drunk with joy
And dance to the rhythms of this song.
Even the mountains and the oceans and
The earth are dancing, while the world of man
Dances in laughter and in tears.
Why would anyone want to take on the role of a monk
And live apart from the world in prideful ego?
Kabir says: Look! My heart is dancing in ecstasy
With all the forms of art, and this makes the Creator smile.

WHAT IS THE NEED OF WORDS?

What is the need of words when your heart is drunk on Love?
I have hidden the Diamond in my coat;
Why do I need to keep unzipping it all the time?
There is no need to even weigh this stone.
The swan has flown to the lake beyond the mountains;
It doesn't need to look for pools and creeks anymore.
The Beloved lives within you.
You don't even need to open your eyes.
Kabir says: Listen, my friend, my Beloved who lives in my eyes
Has united Herself with me.

LIKE THE RIVER FLOWS TO THE OCEAN

How could the love between me and Her ever disappear?
Just like the lotus leaf lives on the water,
So She is my Sovereign and I am Her servant.
Just like the owl gazes all night at the moon,
So She is my Sovereign and I am Her servant.
From the beginning to the end of time,
She is my Sovereign and I am Her servant.
There will always be love between Her and me.
How could anyone or anything extinguish such love?
Kabir says: Just like the river flows to the ocean,
So my heart beats in Her.

THE BATTLEFIELD OF THE BODY

Where is the night when the sun is shining?
And if it is night, then the sun must have taken away its light.
Where there is knowledge, can ignorance survive?
If there is ignorance, then knowledge must die.
If there is lust, how can love be there too?
Where there is Love, there can be no lust.
So fight on, my friend, and give it your best shot.
He who is truly brave never flees from a good fight.
In the battlefield of your body, a great war is going on.
A war against anger, pride, and greed.
It is in the land of Truth and contentment that this battle rages.
This is a hard fight, this fight of the Truth-seeker.
But the Truth-seeker's battle goes on, day and night.
As long as one's life lasts, it never ends.

AT HOME

My Beloved is calling me back home.
I can hear Her.
Only at home is there true union,
And only at home is there true enjoyment of life.
Why would I want to leave home and wander the world?
In truth, there is both bondage and freedom at home.
I long for home, where my mind can think only of Her.
Kabir says: The home is where you must live.
At home there is reality,
And the home helps us to know Her—
Who is more real than reality. So stay where you are,
At home. Everything will come to you in time.

THE BEST KIND OF LOVE

O seeker, the best kind of love is simple. It is free.
Ever since the day when I met my Beloved,
There has been only fun in our love.
I don't close my eyes and I don't close my ears.
I see with my eyes open and with a smile,
And see Her beauty everywhere.
When I speak Her name, everything I see reminds me of Her.
And whatever I do, I am praying to Her,
And all contradictions are solved.
She is my true love. There are no others.
And my lips sing to Her glory both night and day.
I can never forget Her,
For the rhythm of Her music echoes in my ears.
Kabir says: Even if your heart breaks,
Tell Her what you are hiding in your soul.
The Beloved's bliss is greater than all of life's pleasure and pain.

THERE IS NOTHING BUT WATER IN THE POOL

There is nothing but water in the pool where we bathe.
I know that these pools are useless, for I have bathed there.
The images of gods and goddesses near the sacred spring
Are lifeless and cannot speak.
I know, for I have cried out loud to them.
The Vedas and the Koran are only words.
I have lifted up the blanket and have seen what lies beneath.
Kabir says: She who gives voice to the words of experience
Knows without doubt that everything else is not true.

A TREE WITH NO NAME

There is a tree with no name that has no roots
And bears fruit without blossoming.
It has no branches and no leaves, yet is loaded with buds.
There are two birds singing there; one is the Guru
And the other is Her disciple.
The disciple picks the fruits of life and tastes them,
And the Guru watches them and smiles.
What Kabir says will be hard for you to understand:
The bird is beyond seeing, yet it is the bird that we see.
The Formless is a part of all forms, and
I sing, like the bird, to the beauty of forms!

THE WORD

The Word from the universe has come.
That Word is the Beloved.
I have heard it and have become Her disciple.
How many humans are there
Who know the meaning of that word?
O sage, O singer, you must practice that Word!
The Vedas and the Koran say so
And say the whole world is present there.
Even the rishis and converts speak of it,
But none know what it means.
The landowner leaves his land when he hears it.
The ascetic returns to the life of love when he hears it.
The sacred texts of world religions talk about it.
Even the spirit of renunciation points to that Word.
For from that Word, the world we know was created,
And it reveals All.
Kabir says: But no one knows from where the Word does come.

THE OCEAN OF HAPPINESS

When you've come all this way to the ocean of happiness,
Do not return home thirsty with an empty cup.
Wake up! Here is some pure water;
Drink as much as you can!
Do not go looking for a mirage,
But instead look for a pure spring.
Many masters have found the spring
And drank their fill.
And the saints are drunk with love;
Their thirst now is only for love.
Kabir says: Listen to me! The cycle of fear is broken.
With that load of desires in your head,
How can you see the Light?
So hold within you truth, detachment,
And above all: Love.

FREE OF PRIDE AND CONCEIT

O friend, when I was forgetful and lost,
My true Guru showed me the Way.
After that, I gave up all rites and ceremonies,
And I bathed no more in the holy pool.
I learned that it was me who was mad,
And that everything in the world was sane;
And that I was disturbing those who were already wise.
From that time on, I do not ring the bell of the temple.
I do not put an idol on its altar,
And do not worship it with flowers.
The Lord is not pleased when you desecrate your flesh
With ointments and tattoos. Nor when you strip off
Your clothes and numb your senses.
The person who is kind, righteous, and passive
Amidst world affairs and considers all earth creatures
The same as themselves,
It is they who become immortal and are embraced by God.
Kabir says: They who are free of pride and conceit
And whose words are pure attain the status of the Beloved.

OLD HABITS

Get out of here, and go to somewhere where
The friends of the Beloved live.
Take all your "higher thoughts" and love
And get thee hence! Abandon this place
Where Her name is not spoken!
Come on now, tell me how you think you could
Have a wedding feast without the bride.
So, make no more excuses or innocuous plans,
And think only of the Beloved.
And don't start worshipping other gods
Again in this new place, for that is a waste of time.
Kabir says: If you fall back into old habits,
You will never find the Beloved!

Acknowledgments

I'd like to acknowledge John Golebiewski, my editor at Shambhala, and his kind and careful work on this book and with me in such a professional and peaceful way.

I'd like to thank the editorial, design, and marketing teams who put so much faith and time into the beauty and the hoped-for success of this book.

Last but not least, I'd like to give gratitude to the Beloved for the valuable time spent with the wisdom of Kabir and this chance to be of service to All.

About the Author

Thomas Rain Crowe is an internationally published author, editor, and translator of more than thirty books, including the multi-award-winning nature memoir *Zoro's Field: My Life in the Appalachian Woods* (2005); an anthology of contemporary Celtic-language poets titled *Writing the Wind: A Celtic Resurgence* (1997); a collection of original verse, *The Laugharne* Poems, written at the Dylan Thomas Boathouse in Laugharne, Wales (1997); two volumes of translations of the poetry of the Sufi poet Hafiz—*In Wineseller's Street* (Iran Books) and *Drunk on the Wine of the Beloved* (Shambhala Publications); and *The Perfect Work: Poems of Hafiz*, a work of poetry and music (Fern Hill Records, 1999). He has been an editor of major literary and cultural journals and anthologies and is the founder and publisher of New Native Press (www.newnativepress.org). He lived in San Francisco during the 1970s, working alongside the people cited in his book *Starting from San Francisco: The Baby Beat Generation and the Second San Francisco Renaissance* (Third Mind Books, 2018), and was an original member of the group responsible for the resurrection of *Beatitude* magazine during those years. A longtime resident of the southern Appalachians, he lives in the Tuckasegee watershed in the "Little Canada" community of Jackson County in western North Carolina.